I0517367

on Earth as it is

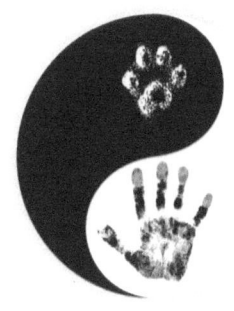

Frank Higgins

haiku

on Earth as it is

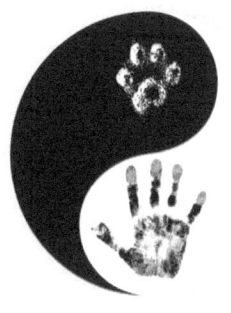

Frank Higgins

haiku

Kansas City — Spartan Press — Missouri

Spartan Press
Kansas City, Missouri

Spartan
Press

Copyright © Frank Higgins 2023
First Edition 1 3 5 7 9 10 8 6 4 2
ISBN: 978-1-958182-26-0
LCCN: 2022949194

Design and Layout: w.e. leathem

Some of these haiku previously appeared in *Frogpond*, *the Haiku Anthology* edited by Cor van den Heuvel, *the Haiku World* anthology edited by William J. Higginson, *Heron's Nest*, the *Kansas City Star*, *Kingfisher*, *the Last Train Home* anthology edited by Jacqueline Pearce, *Modern Haiku, New Letters, Prune Juice, Tsuridoro.*

For Information Contact:

All rights reserved. No part of this publication may be reproduced or transmitted in any form or by any means, electronic or mechanical, including photocopying or recording or by any info retrieval system without the prior written consent of the publisher.

Spring

tank blast
the meadow bursts
with butterflies

root cellar
bulb blooming
toward the knot hole

                    hearing the wren
                    the old woman adds its song
                    to the quilt

still life
taking so long to paint it
the potato sprouts

stopping the talk
of art students
Monet's *Water Lilies*

gorging gulls
more baby turtles
hurry to the sea

spring morning
antlers locked, the elk fight
from their knees

planting corn
the old Navajo sings
to each seed

                    Navajo weaver
          she makes her baby's expression
                    a mask of God

Taos sweat lodge
heating up as one
sung prayers and stone

tornado warning
moths swirling at noon
around the streetlight

tornado shelter
the tot trembles
from daddy long-legs

tornado rubble
a sparrow flies off
with a shoe lace

spring blizzard
bison blowing hot breath
on the new-born

bleeding onstage
the cellist makes her menstrual flow
into music

delta blues
a broken bottle's neck
becomes a bawling baby

on the hardest part
the famous violinist
playing with closed eyes

his fastest riff
the Dixieland jazz pianist
laughing

bayou breakfast
bits of jambalaya
still moving

young pelican
working to swallow a king crab
bigger than itself

the woods still
'til I turn over
a stone

                coyote with a catch
                        the sheep
                   resume grazing

clear-cut mountain
poking out from sawdust
a strawberry—two

first light
the whir of a casting rod
plop

lake outing
the five year old makes friends
in the bait bucket

happy to catch it
the kid now cries—
the trout being cleaned

desert rain
swerving on the highway
for toads in the headlights

                              Get Well gift
                         clogs with the smell
                                      of rain

mid-day downpour
whores in a doorway
share a cigarette

                              rainy night
            for homeless vets the underpass
                    becomes the rally point

inner city school
the cover of the lit book
Sargent's *Madame X*

Holocaust museum
"Not true," says a kid;
"No, it's true, but exaggerated."

another mass shooting
I change the channel
to sports scores

robin egg eaten
the mockingbird adds its song
to the morning

beak-sized bite
of wing missing
the monarch hurries on

prairie burn at night
butterflies fleeing
moths coming

beach cookout
guitars cover the clatter
of crabs on the grill

Chaco Canyon campout
the constellations
lost in the crowd

empty theater
onstage the teenage usher
assumes 1st position

a break from the wind
the prairie trees
still lean

                    desert ruins
           the wind sets off
                a car alarm

tai chi in the park
ten people turn as one
with the wind

Amish country
the plow horse's breath
in the passing headlights

farm family supper
the scent of upturned earth
part of the blessing

morning mist fading
furrow by furrow
the dark earth shines

Summer

summer solstice
a sip from the hose
becomes a guzzle

children in single file
through the puddle
again

helicopter seeds
girls playing tea party
start spinning

the 'hood cools off
the slap of a jump rope
reaches hot peppers

Monument Valley
a hawk's slow circle
in a sonic boom

house cleaning
ants on the desert floor
throw out a shark's tooth

Monument Valley
between gusts
a girl shooting hoops

cliff dwellings
from a crumbling wall
a crow watches us

new scar
the rodeo clown
paints a bigger smile

Wild West Show
the mustang snorts rebellion
for a treat

roadside rattlesnake show
for five bucks the owner's boy
bangs on the wire cage

Amish store
silencing the tourist child
dolls with no faces

Gay Pride Parade
dark hospital windows
fill with faces

Ghost Dancing
in the Dakota fields
missile silos

school's out
a kid pulls crawdads
from their hidey-holes

up late
with the sick child
bugs at the screens

winning at marbles
the challenger even takes
the ex-champ's swagger

winning too much
the girl with Down's glares
over the chessboard

Gettysburg re-enactors
after the volley
no one dies

along Cemetery Ridge
rangers cleaning cannons
of cocoons

where Pickett charged
the four year old wanders
looking for four leaf clovers

Little Round Top
kids on the rocks
playing soldier

small town pool hall
racking them up again
the army recruiter

telling mom I've enlisted
the sound of rice
busy in the pot

as we torch the hut
word comes on the radio
we've walked on the moon

a wolf's long howl
the dog by the campfire
growls at its master

unplanned pregnancy
the mom wrings out a dishrag
to the last drop

Fourth of July
the river reveals
another tire

fireworks
fireflies forgotten
in the jelly jar

home funeral
a boy watches his father
shave *his* father

Arlington
Taps over, the loudest sound
trees

trapped by the screen
the wasp dies
surrounded by air

Texas Panhandle
tread marks in the dust
down Main Street

Rodeo Drive
black woman and white woman
the white one darker

Sunset Boulevard
dreams of walking the red carpet
while walking the street

Walden Pond
through the trees semis
semis semis semis

monastery retreat
watching a cloud cross the pond
instead of stones

above silent monks
a flock of sparrows feeds
on a cloud of gnats

contemplating tao
I scatter bird seed
and start a frenzy

missing evening meal
the abbey's day lilies
closing at dusk

ringing the sacred bell
mixed with the *bong*
angry wasps

before take-off
the chaplin blesses
Enola Gay

hot spell
minnows cool in the shadow
of the heron

among sequoias
how do I ever go back
to grading papers?

long home run
off the guard tower
the crowd silent *

desert wind
pop fly to center
going foul *

called on to pitch
the guard moves his handgun
to the other hip *

*From the sequence "Baseball at Manzanar
Japanese-American Relocation Center 1942-1946"*

T Ball
the right fielder chases
a butterfly

alone on the field
a six year old practices
shaking off the sign

crack of the bat
the Alzheimer's patient
lifts his head

catch with dad
'til neither of us
can see the ball

Autumn

cool breeze
the rusty weather vane
begins to creak

snagged by the bear
the salmon's wound
drips eggs

urban concourse
the one tree's one leaf
begins to lighten

leaf-watching trip—
swerving the car all day
around fuzzy wuzzies

proud of it
the farmer's daughter
with her farmer's tan

farm town high school
in place of hall lockers
hangers and a shelf

harvest time
a storm cloud of starlings
turns inside out

junkyard
through a hot rod chassis
goldenrod

stopping my complaints
about New York
soft light on brownstones

morning sprinkle
finding Central Park
by the sound of frogs

rush hour subway
each face becomes
a Picasso

thunderstorm
from a tenement window
a sax talks back

tenement window
among red geraniums
an old woman's face

murder trial
the defendant's feet
don't reach the floor

brilliant sunset
the distant fire's
death count

mid-day drizzle
at a Times Square tree
the smell of earth

the girl's moves
excite the crowd
Washington Square chess

cold snap
the nave in St Patrick's
smells of hot pretzels

red light
sparrows hurry back to feed
on flattened fries

in the elevator
knowing each neighbor
by cough

filling the front porch
without sounding the wind chimes
evening fog

Golden Gate Bridge
jumpers choose this spot
facing the city

Chinatown fish mart
fillets with red spots
pulsing

tuna boats
included in the catch
all the ocean's colors

war-bound destroyer
dolphins shooting
across the bow

earthquake
above the dark city
the stars brighter

thick morning fog
the comforting clatter
of cable cars

Zen garden
the goldfish grabbed
by a gull

                              pies cooling
                              gramma listens
                              to her times tables

refusing her meds
gramma points at the cures
in the front yard

                              home hospice
                              from the family album
                              gramma names who's who

                  home funeral
          women trade pix of grandkids
            men show pocketknives

October snow
as the first flakes fall
schoolkids' voices rise

duck and cover drill
a girl asks will guns get tired
of looking for us

first grade art fair
afterwards the artist-judge
can't sleep

compact cars
with temporary spares
teachers' parking lot

first frost
this morning mums
dripping red

mountain fog
a bull elk's bugle
finds an answer

layoffs coming
more coins in the wishing well
half of them tails

       factory town
       the school bus driver checks off
       another vacant house

              coal miners off shift
              able to tell who's who
              from who favors what

                     Day of the Dead
                     skull-shaped popsicles
                     turning lips blue

so quietly
the female mantis feeds
from her mate's face

                              visitation
                holding each other's hand
                       a little longer

            at the stoplight
            autumn shows me
         my parents' headstones

scary at last
the front porch jack-o-lantern
full of maggots

gutting the deer
steam mingles
with the mist

thrown on the fire
the log comes alive
with ants

Winter

only a crow
on a winter fence post
prairie from the train

winter walk
not hearing the silence
until the squish

off-season
from the stone bridge
deer hooves clatter

not feeling winter
till taking out a tip
for the street musician

below freezing
sound of a basketball
in the city park

listening to Lennon
my shelf of must-read books
gets shorter

night drive through Big Sur
the surf—or is it sirens—
whispers

dog on the bed
protection from intruders
that come in dreams

frosted windows
the sermon hot enough
to speak in tongues

high school job fair
the line for Armed Services
wraps around college

steel mill town
downwind from the smokestacks
black icicles

slave cemetery
under the magnolias
unnamed graves

deep South
no cars but I still signal
to change lanes

sub-zero
the soup kitchen head nun's
silent head count

skid row
wind in an empty bottle
leads to another man

women's shelter
new clothes
same eyes

under a railroad bridge
a ragged man
adding his name

outside the job bank
men around an oil drum fire
make room for one more

into the tunnel
we see ourselves
and turn away

psych ward
above the Christmas Muzak
a long cry

evening rounds
darkness drops in
to say remember me

swirling clouds
Van Gogh's asylum paintings
making sense

four below
nothing moves on the river
but the full moon

Christmas reunion
the vet sits while nephews fight
to use his crutches

returned vet
sleeping on the floor
of his old room

Christmas AA meeting
the sound of more metal chairs
dragged in

outstate Montana
strangers in on-coming cars
wave

saddle store
the cowboys speak
as though in church

finally a kill
the hunter warms his hands
with the pheasant

at the museum
tourists in front of *The Scream*
laughing at selfies

dead child on the street
the neighbor screams beside it
holding her nose

desert night
the five year old says, "What if
those aren't stars but holes?"

watching the news
the mother-to-be
caresses her stomach

prison poetry class
an inmate writing
tongue out

the inmate's rap
about finding Christ
written in crayon

brick-sized window
the distance between
his cell and the moon

at my mom's deathbed—
we watch a coming rain cloud
till the pane is wet

under the redwoods
I remember
this life will end

(for Robert Epstein)

winter morning
child and dog at the window
noses to the glass

almost spring
pantry shelves full
with empty mason jars

the goose's foot
falls through the ice—
winter's end

mother and daughter
buying bus tickets out of town
with nickels and dimes

Frank Higgins is a playwright and poet. His plays *Black Pearl Sings!, The Sweet By'n'By* and *Gunplay: A Play About America,* which had scenes read on Capitol Hill, have been produced around the country. His plays for young audiences include *The Country of the Blind,* an adaptation of the story by H.G. Wells. As a poet he has published the books *Starting From Ellis Island* and *American Haiku* and *Eating Blowfish.* He taught for many years in the Young Audiences' program Artists-in-the-Schools in Missouri and Kansas. He teaches playwriting at the University of Missouri-Kansas City, and is a member of the Dramatists Guild, and the Haiku Society of America.

www.ingramcontent.com/pod-product-compliance
Lightning Source LLC
Chambersburg PA
CBHW031246120626
46545CB00007B/2670